Selling Out

John Goodwin

Published in association with
The Basic Skills Agency

Hodder & Stoughton

A MEMBER OF THE HODDER HEADLINE GROUP

Acknowledgements
Cover: Mark Preston
Illustrations: Doug Gray

Orders: please contact Bookpoint Ltd, 130 Milton Park, Abingdon, Oxon OX14 4SB. Telephone: (44) 01235 827720, Fax: (44) 01235 400454. Lines are open from 9.00 – 6.00, Monday to Saturday, with a 24 hour message answering service. You can also order through our website: www.hodderheadline.co.uk

British Library Cataloguing in Publication Data
A catalogue record for this title is available from The British Library

ISBN 0 340 87628 X

First published 2001
This edition published 2002
Impression number   10 9 8 7 6 5 4 3 2 1
Year   2007 2006 2005 2004 2003 2002

Typeset by SX Composing DTP, Rayleigh, Essex.
Printed in Great Britain for Hodder & Stoughton Educational, 338 Euston Road, London NW1 3BH by Athenaeum Press, Gateshead, Tyne and Wear.

About the play

The People
- **Ravi**, a young football player
- **Joe**, a young football player
- **Danny**, a young football player
- **Benny**, the coach
- **The Football Crowd**
- **The Referee**

The Place
Sutton United Youth Football Club

What's Happening
Ravi, **Joe** *and* **Danny** *are playing a football match.*
Benny *looks on from the touch line.*

Act 1

Scene 1

Crowd	UNITED! UNITED!
Joe	Pass it.
Ravi	Pass the ball.
Benny	Pass the ball, Danny. Pass it to Ravi.
Joe	Yeah.
Benny	Well done, Danny.
Joe	Great pass, Danny.
Benny	Now go for it, Ravi.
Danny	Go for goal.
Crowd	GIVE US A GOAL! GIVE US A GOAL!
Joe	Man on Ravi.
Benny	Look out, Ravi.
Danny	Man on Ravi!

The Referee blows a whistle for a foul on Ravi.

Benny	Foul!
Joe	You dirty fouler.
Crowd	SEND HIM OFF.
	SEND HIM OFF.
Benny	Don't move, Ravi.
	I'll be with you.
Ravi	I think I've broken my leg.
Benny	Easy now.
Ravi	The pain's terrible.
Referee	We'll need a stretcher.
	I'll blow my whistle for half time.
	The Referee blows the whistle.

Scene 2

Half time on the pitch.
Ravi has been taken to hospital.

Danny	Do you think he'll be OK, Benny?
Benny	Yes.
Joe	Do you reckon his leg is broken?
Benny	We've got to forget about Ravi.
Danny	We can't forget about him.
Benny	We have to.
	Think about the game.
	We're one–nil ahead.
	Danny, play in defence.
Danny	Right.
Benny	All of you, play hard.
	Don't let in any soft goals, Joe.
	Keep your eye on the ball.
Joe	Right.
Benny	We can still win this one.

	The Referee's whistle goes for the start of the second half.
Crowd	UNITED.
	UNITED.
	IF YOU ALL LIKE UNITED
	CLAP YOUR HANDS.
	IF YOU ALL LIKE UNITED
	CLAP YOUR HANDS.
	IF YOU ALL LIKE UNITED
	IF YOU ALL LIKE UNITED
	IF YOU ALL LIKE UNITED
	CLAP YOUR HANDS.
Benny	Come on United.
	Watch their number nine.
Joe	Look out, defence.
Benny	Look out, Joe.
Joe	Tackle him, Danny.
Benny	He's through our defence.
Joe	Tackle him.
Benny	He's going for goal.
Joe	He's in the penalty area.
Benny	Tackle him, Danny.
Joe	Tackle him, Danny.

Benny	Not like that!

The Referee's whistle blows for a foul.

Referee	That was a foul.
	A dirty foul.
Benny	Come off it, Ref.
Referee	Yellow card.
Danny	What?
Referee	Penalty.
Benny	Not a penalty, Ref.

The Referee's whistle blows for the penalty.

Referee	Penalty to Rovers.
Danny	It's all my fault.
Benny	You've got to save it, Joe.
Joe	Which way will he shoot?
Danny	Come on, Joe.

Crowd	COME ON JOE
	COME ON JOE
Joe	He's going to shoot to the right.
Danny	He's scored . . .
	No he hasn't.
	Joe's . . .
Benny	Saved it.
Crowd	WHAT A SAVE
	WHAT A SAVE
Benny	Great save, Joe.
Danny	Well done, Joe.
Benny	You've saved the game.
Crowd	UNITED
	UNITED
	WHAT A WIN
	WHAT A WIN

The Referee's whistle goes for the end of the match. Everybody cheers.

Act 2

In Benny's office. Six weeks later.
Ravi *comes into the office on crutches.*

Benny	How goes it, Ravi?
Ravi	Terrible.
Benny	Why's that?
Ravi	It hurts worse than when I did it.
Benny	You should take it easy.
Ravi	I can't take it easy.
	I can't sleep at nights.
	For six long weeks it's been like this.
Benny	That's bad news.
Ravi	Yes.
Benny	The team miss you.
Ravi	I miss football.
Benny	So when is it going to get better?
Ravi	I don't know.
	Sometimes it seems like
	I'll never play again.

Benny	You're too good a player to miss so many games.
Ravi	I just wish it would get better.
Benny	How much do you wish?
Ravi	What?
Benny	I said, how much do you wish your leg was better?
Ravi	You know how much.
Benny	Yes I do. I might have something to help you.
Ravi	What?
Benny	Something from Benny's top drawer.

Benny *opens the top drawer of his desk and takes out a small packet. He gives it to* **Ravi**.

	A few of these should sort you out.
Ravi	What are they?
Benny	Don't ask questions, Ravi.
Ravi	Just tell me what they are.
Benny	A little something to build up your muscles.
Ravi	Oh yeah?

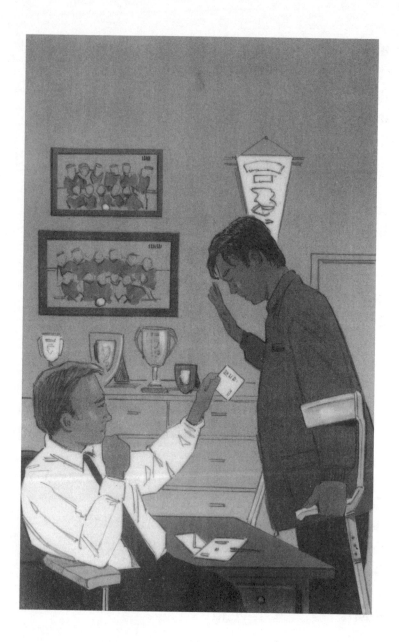

Benny	To help build up your muscles so you can get back in the game soon. Take a few of those and you could be playing in a few weeks. Just think of that, Ravi.
Ravi	They're drugs, aren't they? I don't want any drugs.
Benny	They're harmless.
Ravi	No they're not. I know what these are . . . they are steroid drugs. Athletes take these, then get banned for life.
Benny	They're nothing like that. Do you want to play again this season, Ravi?
Ravi	Of course I want to play again this season. I can do it without drugs.
Benny	Are you sure of that?
Ravi	Yes.

Act 3

At Ravi's house. A few weeks later.

Danny   So we won three–nil.

Ravi   Oh.

Danny   Elroy's taken your
position as striker.
He had a great match.
He scored two brilliant goals.

Ravi   Oh.

Danny   How's your leg?

Ravi   Not much better.

Danny   You should come up
and see us play.
We're going to win
the league this year.

Ravi   Really?

Danny   So are you going to
come and see the next match?

Ravi   I'll see.

Act 4

In Benny's office.

Joe	You wanted to see me.
Benny	Yes. Take a seat, Joe.
Joe	OK.
Benny	You've been playing goalie really well the last few months.
Joe	The whole team have been playing like a dream.
Benny	Yes.
Joe	Ten goals in three matches can't be bad.
Benny	But you've made some blinding saves, Joe. None better than saving that penalty. That was brilliant.
Joe	Bit of luck.
Benny	More than luck, Joe.
Joe	Not really.

Benny	We are six points clear
	at the top of the league.
Joe	With a game in hand.
Benny	So we can relax a bit.
Joe	You can never relax in football.

Benny *opens his top drawer and pulls out an envelope.*

Benny	Something for you, Joe.
Joe	For me?
Benny	A present for being a
	brilliant goalie. Open it.

Joe *opens the envelope.*

Joe	A load of cash.
Benny	A hundred quid to be exact.
Joe	A hundred quid!
Benny	You've got real talent.
	Talent to go to the very top.
Joe	I can't take this.
Benny	You'll get to the top
	and learn to take presents.
Joe	What do you mean?
Benny	Take the cash and maybe . . .

17

Joe	Maybe what?
Benny	Maybe relax a bit the next game.
	It wouldn't matter if you let
	in a couple of goals.
	Just for the next match.
Joe	You want me to let in goals.
Benny	Got it in one.
Joe	Why?
Benny	I need us to lose the match.
Joe	What for?
Benny	There's money in this. Big money.
Joe	You want me to fix the match.
	Well I'm not going to.
	No way. Keep your cash.
Benny	Don't be in such a rush.
	Think about it.
	You could use a hundred quid,
	couldn't you?
	And that's just for starters.
	There'll be more in the future.
Joe	You don't bribe me.
Benny	Steady, Joe.
	I can easily find another goalie.
	Just think about it.

Act 5

Scene 1

At Ravi's house.

Ravi   He offered me drugs.
Joe   He didn't.
Ravi   He did.
Joe   You didn't take them?
Ravi   No.
          But I was tempted.
          Hobbling about on crutches
          week after week isn't much fun.
          I was thinking about giving them
          a try.
Joe   He offered me cash.
Ravi   What for?
Joe   For fixing a game.
Ravi   You didn't take it.

Joe	No. But just think what you could buy with a hundred quid. And there'd be a load more dosh to follow. All I had to do was say yes.
Ravi	One simple little word.
Joe	We've got to stop him.
Ravi	How?
Joe	Shop him.
Ravi	How are we going to do that then?
Joe	I know exactly how we'll do it. You and I are going to pay Benny a visit in his office.

Scene 2

In Benny's office.

Joe	So we've been thinking it over.
Benny	Sounds good to me, boys.
Ravi	Yeah, I reckon those steroids will do the trick. I mean, you did want me to take them Benny, didn't you?
Benny	Of course I did, Ravi.
Ravi	Even though they are illegal.
Benny	Ravi . . . everybody needs to bend the rules now and again don't they? That's all we are doing.
Joe	I could really use a hundred quid right now, Benny.
Benny	Of course you could.
Joe	Just to let in a goal or two. I mean, every goalie has an off day now and then.
Benny	Of course they do.

Joe	So you're going to pay me a hundred quid to lose a few games for you? So you can do a dodgy deal and win a few bets. Have I got it right, Benny?
Benny	You got it in one. I can let you have the money right now.
Ravi	Drugs and bribes.
Benny	That's putting it a bit strong, Ravi.
Ravi	Is it?
Benny	This is just to help you two lads out.
Joe	Really?
Ravi	Make me a junkie . . . that's helping me out, is it?
Joe	And make me take a bribe to lose a game. What kind of sportsman would do that?

Benny	What's going on?
Ravi	We're going to shop you, Benny.
Joe	Let everybody know
	the truth about you.
Benny	Oh really?
Ravi	Yes.
Joe	Yes.
Benny	You've got no proof.
	Nobody will believe two kids.

| Joe | But we have got proof. |
| | Show him the recorder, Ravi. |

Ravi *takes a small tape recorder out of his pocket.*

| Ravi | It's all here. Listen. |

Ravi *rewinds the tape and plays back the conversation.*

Joe	We've got you taped, Benny.
	Clear evidence.
Benny	Nobody is going to believe you.
	You're just two kids.
Joe	Eleven kids actually, Benny.
Ravi	Yes.

Joe	Eleven kids and one tape recorder.
	All the evidence we need
	to prove that
	you offered drugs.
Ravi	Or tried to bribe us.
Joe	There's no way out.
Ravi	No place to hide.
Joe	No place in football for you.
Ravi	You're finished, Benny.
Crowd	UNITED
	UNITED

The whistle goes for the end of the match.

If you have enjoyed reading this book, you may be interested in other titles in the *Livewire* series.

The Library
Romeo, Romeo
Doing Macbeth
Night Fishing
Place Your Bets

The Mimic
Football Clones
The Day Trippers
The Chosen One

Speedway
Rider

John Goodwin

Published in association with
The Basic Skills Agency

Acknowledgements
Cover: Stuart Williams
Illustrations: Joan Corlass

Orders; please contact Bookpoint Ltd, 39 Milton Park, Abingdon, Oxon OX14 4TD. Telephone: (44) 01235 400414, Fax: (44) 01235 400454. Lines are open from 9.00–6.00, Monday to Saturday, with a 24 hour message answering service. Email address: orders@bookpoint.co.uk

British Library Cataloguing in Publication Data
A catalogue record for this title is available from the British Library

ISBN 0 340 77610 2

First published 2000
Impression number 10 9 8 7 6 5 4 3 2 1
Year   2005 2004 2003 2002 2001 2000

Typeset by GreenGate Publishing Services, Tonbridge, Kent.
Printed in Great Britain for Hodder and Stoughton Educational, a division of Hodder Headline Plc, 338 Euston Road, London NW1 3BH, by Atheneum Press, Gateshead, Tyne & Wear